W9-BIU-707

When an American says that he loves his country, he means not only that he loves the New England hills, the prairies glistening in the sun, the wide and rising plains, the great mountains and the sea. He means that he loves an inner air, an inner light in which freedom lives and in which a man can draw the breath of self-respect.

Adlai Stevenson

March 1976

Sharry L. Beadling
532 - East Milner
Alliance 44601

FOR ~
SUSAN AND JEFFREY HARRICK

One flag, one land, one heart, one
*   hand,*
One nation, evermore!
*   Oliver Wendell Holmes*

AMERICA
THE BEAUTIFUL
('O BEAUTIFUL FOR SPACIOUS SKIES')

Hymn by
Katharine Lee Bates

The C. R. Gibson Company, *Publishers*
Norwalk, Connecticut

O beautiful for spacious skies,
  For amber waves of grain,
For purple mountain majesties
  Above the fruited plain!

. . . my cup runneth over.
  Surely goodness and mercy shall follow
me all the days of my life: and I will
dwell in the house of the Lord for ever.
Psalm 23:5, 6

I hear America singing,
The varied carols I hear . . .
    Walt Whitman

. . . Be fruitful, and multiply, and replenish
the earth, and subdue it: and have
dominion over the fish of the sea, and
over the fowl of the air, and over every
living thing that moveth upon the earth.
Genesis 1:28

America is a land of wonders, in which
everything is in constant motion and every
change an improvement . . . No natural
boundary seems to be set to the efforts
of man, and in his eyes what is not yet
done is only what he has not yet attempted
to do.
    Alexis de Tocqueville

America! America!
God shed his grace on thee,
And crown thy good
with brotherhood
From sea to shining sea!

Let brotherly love continue.
Be not forgetful to entertain strangers:
for thereby some have entertained angels
unawares.

Hebrews 13:1-2

The United States themselves are
essentially the greatest poem . . . Here at
last is something in the doings of man
that corresponds with the broadcast doings
of the day and night.

Walt Whitman

And so, my fellow Americans, ask not
what your country can do for you; .
ask what you can do for your country.

John F. Kennedy

O beautiful for pilgrim feet,
  Whose stern, impassioned stress
A thoroughfare for freedom beat
  Across the wilderness!

So at last I was going to America!
Really, really going, at last! The boundaries
burst. The arch of heaven soared. A
million suns shone out for every star.
The winds rushed in from outer space,
roaring in my ears, "America! America!"
                                    Mary Antin

Land where my fathers died
Land of the pilgrims' pride,
From every mountainside
Let freedom ring.
Samuel Francis Smith

Being thus arrived in a good harbor,
and brought safe to land, they [the
pilgrims] fell upon their knees and blessed
the God of Heaven who had brought
them over the vast and furious ocean,
and delivered them from all the perils and
miseries thereof, again to set their feet
upon the firm and stable earth . . .
William Bradford

America! America!
God mend thine every flaw,
Confirm thy soul in self-control,
Thy liberty in law!

The God who gave us life, gave us liberty
at the same time.

Thomas Jefferson

The basis of our political system is the
right of the people to make and to alter
their constitutions of government.

George Washington

God grants liberty only to those who love
it, and are always ready to guard and
defend it.

Daniel Webster

Is life so dear or peace so sweet as to be
purchased at the price of chains and
slavery? Forbid it, Almighty God.
I know not what course others may take,
but as for me, give me liberty or give
me death!

Patrick Henry

We must scrupulously guard the . . . civil
liberties of all citizens. We must remember
that any oppressions, any injustice, any
hatred is a wedge designed to attack
our civilization.

Franklin Delano Roosevelt

Give me your tired, your poor,
Your huddled masses yearning to breathe free,
The wretched refuse of your teeming shore,
Send these, the homeless, tempest-tossed, to me;
I lift my lamp beside the golden door.
Emma Lazarus

Here rests in honored glory an American
soldier known but to God.
Inscription, Tomb of the Unknown Soldier

... that we here highly resolve that these
dead shall not have died in vain; that
this nation, under God, shall have a new
birth of freedom ...

Abraham Lincoln

The fate of unborn millions will now
depend, under God, on the courage and
conduct of this army ...

George Washington

Hail, Columbia! happy land!
Hail, ye heroes! heaven-born band!
Who fought and bled in Freedom's cause.
Hail, Columbia!

Joseph Hopkinson

I have not yet begun to fight.

John Paul Jones

O beautiful for heroes proved
    In liberating strife,
Who more than self their
        country loved,
And mercy more than life!

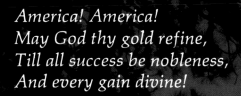

America! America!
May God thy gold refine,
Till all success be nobleness,
And every gain divine!

Let us contemplate our forefathers, and
posterity, and resolve to maintain the
rights bequeathed to us from the former,
for the sake of the latter.

Samuel Adams

I have sworn upon the altar of God,
eternal hostility against every form of
tyranny over the mind of man.
                    Thomas Jefferson

Far better it is to dare mighty things,
to win glorious triumphs, even though
checkered by failure, than to take rank
with those poor spirits who neither enjoy
much or suffer much, because they live
in the gray twilight that knows neither
victory nor defeat.
                    Theodore Roosevelt

O beautiful for patriot dream
That sees beyond the years,

We fight not to enslave, but to set a
country free, and to make room upon the
earth for honest men to live in.
Thomas Paine

Don't one of you fire until you see the
whites of their eyes.
William Prescott, at Bunker Hill

Our country, right or wrong. When right,
to be kept right; when wrong, to be
put right.
Carl Schurz

Territory is but the body of a nation.
The people who inhabit its hills and valleys
are its soul, its spirit, its life.
James Garfield

. . . they shall beat their swords into plow-
shares, and their spears into pruninghooks:
nation shall not lift up sword against
nation, neither shall they learn war any
more.
Isaiah 2:4

Thine alabaster cities gleam,
Undimmed by human tears!

America is God's crucible, the great
melting pot where all the races . . . are
melting and reforming.

Israel Zangwill

Hog butcher for the world,
Tool maker, stacker of wheat,
Player with railroads and the nation's
    freight handler;
Stormy, husky, brawling,
City of the big shoulders.

Carl Sandburg, Chicago

Except the Lord build the house, they
labour in vain that build it: except the Lord
keep the city, the watchman waketh but
in vain.

Psalms 127:1

America! America!
God shed his grace on thee,

So it's home again, and home again,
    America for me,
My heart is turning home again, and
    there I long to be.

                    Henry van Dyke

I love thy rocks and rills,
Thy woods and templed hills;
My heart with rapture thrills
  Like that above.

Samuel Francis Smith

The land was ours before we were the
  land's.
She was our land more than a hundred
  years
Before we were her people.

Robert Frost

It is a fabulous country, the only fabulous
country; it is the only place where
miracles not only happen, but where they
happen all the time.

Thomas Wolfe

And crown thy good
with brotherhood
From sea to shining sea!

America lives in the heart of every man everywhere who wishes to find a region where he will be free to work out his destiny as he chooses.

Woodrow Wilson

For this truth must be clear before us; whatever America hopes to bring in the world must first come to pass in the heart of America.

Dwight D. Eisenhower

God grant that not only the love of liberty,
but a thorough knowledge of the rights
of man may pervade all nations of the
earth so that a philosopher may set his foot
anywhere on its surface and say, "This
is my country."

Benjamin Franklin

Amen.

We hold these truths to be self-evident;
that all men are created equal; that they
are endowed by their creator with certain
unalienable rights; that among these are
life, liberty, and the pursuit of happiness.
The Declaration of Independence

American liberty is a religion. It is a thing
of the spirit. It is an aspiration on the
part of the people for not alone a free life,
but a better one.
Wendell L. Willkie

To what avail the plow or sail,
Or land, or life, if freedom fail?
Ralph Waldo Emerson

He loved his country as no other man has
loved her, but no man deserved less at
her hands.
Edward Everett Hale,
The Man Without a Country

Our country is the world — our country-
men are all mankind.
William Lloyd Garrison

I have fallen in love with American names.
The sharp names that never get fat,
The snakeskin titles of mining claims,
The plumed war bonnet of Medicine Hat,
Tucson and Deadwood and Lost Mule Flat.
                    Stephen Vincent Benét

O Beautiful for Spacious Skies

KATHARINE LEE BATES, 1859-1929

MATERNA CMD
SAMUEL A. WARD, 1847-1903

1. O beau - ti - ful for spa - cious skies, For am - ber waves of grain,
2. O beau - ti - ful for pil - grim feet, Whose stern, im - pas - sioned stress
3. O beau - ti - ful for he - roes proved In lib - er - at - ing strife,
4. O beau - ti - ful for pa - triot dream That sees be - yond the years

For pur - ple moun - tain maj - es - ties A - bove the fruit - ed plain!
A thor - ough - fare for free - dom beat A - cross the wil - der - ness!
Who more than self their coun - try loved, And mer - cy more than life!
Thine al - a - bas - ter cit - ies gleam, Un - dimmed by hu - man tears!

A - mer - i - ca! A - mer - i - ca! God shed his grace on thee,
A - mer - i - ca! A - mer - i - ca! God mend thine ev - ery flaw,
A - mer - i - ca! A - mer - i - ca! May God thy gold re - fine,
A - mer - i - ca! A - mer - i - ca! God shed his grace on thee,

And crown thy good with broth - er - hood From sea to shin - ing sea.
Con - firm thy soul in self - con - trol, Thy lib - er - ty in law.
Till all suc - cess be no - ble - ness, And ev - ery gain di - vine.
And crown thy good with broth - er - hood From sea to shin - ing sea. A - men.